Blogging
for
Beginners

Learn How to Start and Maintain
a Successful Blog the Simple Way

By Terence Lawfield

Published in Canada

© Copyright 2015 – Terence Lawfield

ISBN-13: 978-1507653395
ISBN-10: 1507653395

Table of Contents

Introduction

In recent years, 'Blogging' has become one of the most widely used words on the internet and in books. In this book, we will explore many facets of blogging which will help to kick-start your goal of becoming a success story in blogging or at least familiarize yourself with this new internet craze.

This is an ultimate beginner's guide to blogging because it starts where other books never start. In this book, I do not make assumptions about what the reader knows. First, we will explore exactly what a blog is. You cannot start a blog if you do not know what it is! We will then discuss several reasons why different people start blogging, from wanting to get their voice out to the masses, to establishing a profitable business venture. As we delve further into the topic, this book will introduce you to the many different types of blogs that you can start when you begin your journey, and then we will discuss the ingredients of a good blog. Lastly, we will explore the technicalities of setting up a blog and how to promote and monetize your new blog.

Chapter 1:
What is Blogging and why do People Blog?

The word 'blog' is the shortened form of the word 'weblog' or 'web log.' These two words can be used interchangeably, although you do not normally see people using the word weblog nowadays. Generally, a blog is an online diary or journal. It is your own personal website that you can update with new content and material whenever you like. With your blog, you are able to share your dreams, your thoughts and your passions to the world. However, blogging is not exclusive to individuals; many companies have blogs as well.

There is some common terminology used in the world of blogging, and it would be beneficial for you to familiarize yourself with it as it will be used a lot throughout the book. 'To blog' means to write a blog. A 'blogger' is a person who maintains a blog, or someone who blogs. Finally, 'blogging' is the act of writing a blog.

Now that you have the terminology down, let's explore the reasons why people write a blog.

Reasons for Blogging

The main question running through your head at this point is likely, "Why on Earth would I want to blog? Why share my dreams and passions with the world when I could just write them in a book?" Although each person starts a blog for a different reason, your reason will probably fall into one of the following categories.

To help people

Many blogs today are set up to help people. For example, there are many parenting blogs meant to provide advice to new parents as well as parents of teenagers and pre-teens. These blogs can work in a therapeutic way for people who need the help, and it makes them aware that they are not the only person going through that particular problem.

To make money

There are many ways that you can use your blog to make money. For instance, you could use it for selling a product or service or even to promote other people's products. The possibilities are endless. You just need to know exactly how to approach it.

To market or self-promote

Many businesses use blogging as a means of promoting their products and services and gaining an online business presence. Blogs can be used as a medium for sharing tutorials with customers, answering frequently asked questions and also advertising new releases. Blogs can also be used by businesses to share customer reviews of their products or to provide exclusive discounts and promotions.

Additionally, in the same way that businesses can use blogs to market their products and services, professionals can use blogs to market themselves and leave a mark in their field of work.

To satisfy creativity and have fun

Blogging can be a way to unleash your creative side. Sometimes our minds are filled with new ideas but we are unsure of them, afraid to share them with close friends and family for fear of rejection or just need a second opinion. Blogging is also very fun for some people. It is a favorite pastime of many who have a sheer passion for the act of blogging itself.

To stay in touch, create records keep private online journals

Blogs can provide an easy way for friends and family to stay in touch from different parts of the world. A friend or family from across the world can just look at your blog, read your posts and see exactly what is going on in your life.

Blogs can also be used to create records of important events in our everyday lives. Blogs are an excellent way to perpetuate important events and memories in your life because they will be available forever unless you decide to take them down.

In just the same way that blogs can be used to keep records of important events, they can be used to store events from your daily life. You may use your blog to store your private thoughts, feelings and opinions and make it inaccessible to everyone else. In this way, it will literally be your virtual diary. To do this, you can grant permissions to a specific set of people while blocking everyone else from accessing your blog.

To make a difference

Blogs are excellent tools, which can be used to sway public opinion on certain matters of interest. For example, many politicians use blogs as a vehicle to encourage readers to participate in politics and to engage people in a variety of advocacy efforts.

To express thoughts and opinions

One of the main reasons why people blog nowadays is to express their thoughts and their opinions on a variety of topics. Some people just want to be heard, and blogging is a great way to spread ideas and make new connections with like-minded people from all across the world.

Before you begin blogging, you will need to choose the type of blog you wish to create. The following section discusses the different types of blogs you can choose from.

8

Chapter 2:
Types of Blogs

Niche Expert Blogs

Niche blogs are set up to make money. The main goal of a niche blogger is to create content, which will be valuable for a certain set of people and are frequently used as a passive income stream. They are usually very targeted and they have strong on-page Search Engine Optimization (SEO) which helps to bring in visitors quickly. Profits and commissions can then be made from the purchases and clicks of the visitors.

Business Blogs

A business blog is meant to have high quality content on different areas of interest for customers to read. Business blogs can be about almost any topic but they are always related to the core of the business that is being marketed. As such, they usually provide high quality information that gives customers the information that they actually care about. This, in effect, draws even more visitors to their businesses website, making it more of a marketing mechanism.

Professional Blogs

Professional blogs are hybrids of business blogs and niche expert blogs. Usually, the creators write about topics that they love and are knowledgeable in, and the blog itself is also an essential aspect of their business. Professional bloggers make money by many different means. There are usually not many advertisements or affiliate links on their sites. Instead, professional bloggers use their sites to promote their own eBooks, courses, subscription services, consulting and other digital products that they have made. These businesses usually do not have an offline presence, but you will find high quality content on these sites because this content is an important part of their business.

Journals

Journals are usually written in a narrative style and are more informal in nature. Authors of journals usually write about a variety of topics, much like how one would write in a traditional diary. Some may have a large number of readers depending on how long they have been blogging for and the nature of the topic they blog about. Journals are not usually set up for profit but are merely a means for creative outlet or having fun. The authors of journals usually post content frequently, often daily or every two days.

Branding Blogs

Branding blogs are set up by people who want to make a name for themselves as experts in their fields before they start seeking monetary gain from the blog. As such, they usually shy away from short-term advertising, and their blogs are not usually filled with affiliate links and advertisements. Their content is usually of high quality.

Promotional Blogs

These blogs are usually written by those who are selling a new book or new product. You will not usually find them on a single blog but rather, they will 'guest post' for several different blogs. Sometimes, these bloggers do not even have a blog site of their own. They simply exist through postings about their products on other sites and through interviews.

Knowing the type of blog to choose and actually succeeding as a blogger are two different elements. Therefore, we must explore the qualities of successful bloggers that you should embrace if you wish to be successful.

Chapter 3:
The Qualities of a Successful Blogger

Now that you know what blogging is, why people blog, and the types of blogs available, you are likely asking yourself, "Do I really have what it takes to be a good blogger? What really are the qualities of a successful blogger?" The qualities described below are assets that all successful bloggers have in common.

Passion

To be a successful blogger, you must be passionate about what you do. Whether you use blogging as a means to express your creative side or as a means to disseminate information, you need to love and be passionate about doing it if you want to be successful. It is this love and passion that will give you the drive to continue blogging, especially when you are just starting and there are not a lot of people visiting your blog. If you keep blogging and working at it, however, you will soon be able to generate a lot of traffic because your readers will identify with whatever you are blogging about. They will also feel the passion that you have for the topic and be motivated to share the posts as well.

Dedication

It is possible for you to be passionate about your blog and the topic that you write about but still not be dedicated to the actual writing. If you are serious about blogging, you have to show dedication and blog on a regular basis. Even if you are able to write the most moving post, if your subscribers see that you are not posting regularly, they will stop visiting regularly until they eventually stop visiting altogether. A successful blogger has to be dedicated to the task at hand and creative as well. Coming up with new content on a regular basis is not an easy task, but it can be done. It simply requires a lot of dedication and hard work.

Knowledge about your topics of interest and desire to learn more

In order to write engaging posts that are both informative and fun to read, a blogger must have extensive knowledge or experience in the specific topic at hand. No one will subscribe to a blog that they know is providing erroneous or deficient information. Therefore, a blogger should ensure that he or she is well-informed about the topic he or she is writing about.

A good blogger must also be willing to learn new information about the particular topic that they write about. No one knows everything about any particular topic, and at some point in time, a blogger is going to have to do research so that he or she can churn out new content that subscribers will love.

Ability to write quality content

Even if you are the most passionate and prolific writer of all time, all of your efforts will likely go to waste if you are unable to bring the content across in an informative and engaging way. You should create content that is different and stands out from the crowd. This is the type of content that people are always willing to share, bookmark, tweet, mark as a favorite and follow, and it is bound to build you a large following in the process.

Good marketing skills

A successful blogger knows how to promote his or her blog without coming across as annoying. There is a delicate balance between effective marketing increases traffic to your blog, and annoying marketing that spams people's emails. Constantly asking people to read and share new posts will only put people off, and you will end up getting less traffic to your blog. A more effective way of marketing includes asking close friends to share your posts so that they gain a wider audience as well as writing guest posts for other bloggers, with links to your own blog.

Thick skinned

To succeed in the world of blogging, one must learn to be impervious to criticisms. There will be many instances where people will disagree with what you write and some will voice their opinions in the harshest and cruelest way possible. As such, you need to learn to accept opposing views, and if you need to respond, you should do so respectfully. This will show your level of professionalism, and it will gain the admiration of many of your subscribers who will respect you for your composed and mature response.

Helpfulness

Helping fellow bloggers and subscribers in the blogosphere where possible will, in turn, help you succeed in the blogging world. If you want people to share your posts, start sharing other people's posts. It is a subtle way of asking people to promote your posts as well. You should also try to help your subscribers. Respond to comments made on your blog as much as possible, and answer questions when you can. This is a great way of making your blog more interactive for everyone. Subscribers are more likely to share your posts with their friends and family when they feel that they are important to you and your blog. Make your subscribers feel needed by responding to their posts regularly and respectfully.

SEO Knowledge

If you want to be an effective blogger, you need to learn some SEO as this is what will help you promote your website on the search engines. Ultimately, it will be significantly easier to attain your blogging goals when you have more people visiting your blog after searching for a certain keyword on the search engines.

Organization and good time management

Blogging requires time and effort so you need to have the discipline to research on what to write about, write high quality posts, promote your posts and even engage your audience. All of these necessities require time and effort, therefore making it critical for you to plan your time wisely.

Now that you have a basic understanding of what makes a good blogger, you should be ready to start a blog. To get started, you need to know the ingredients of a blog, which we will explore first before we delve into the more complex elements of setting it up

Chapter 4:
Ingredients for a Blog

After reading the previous chapter, you might have determined that you do have the qualities of a good blogger or that you can develop these qualities to succeed. So now the big question in your mind is probably, "How can I set up my own blog?" Here are some essential ingredients to get started.

Niche

As mentioned before, niche blogging is creating a blog in such a way that it can be promoted to a niche market. A niche market is a focused and targetable subsection of a market that has a particular need that you, the blogger, can fill. You have a competitive advantage when you are able to fill the needs of a niche market as a specialist.

You need to research extensively to determine if the niche you are choosing is, indeed, profitable. It makes little sense to blog for a niche market that only receives a few monthly searches. Instead, you should try to find a topic with many searches per month and relatively low competition. This is very important because, if you settle for a niche that has a lot of searches but is filled with other established bloggers, it is highly unlikely that you will be able to profit from that niche. Think of it like competing with an established chain store in your neighborhood. Most people will want to visit the recognized and well-established store!

To help you settle on a profitable yet less competitive niche, or even a subgroup of that niche (i.e. micro niche), keyword research is critical. You can use **Word Tracker** or and even **Google's Keyword Planner** to try and gauge the number of searches that a keyword gets each month and to see the amount of competition for that keyword. If it has a relatively high number of searches with few results, then you have found yourself a profitable niche market.

After finding a profitable niche market, the next step is to set up the blog. To do this, you need a domain name for your blog, and from there, the next step is webhosting it. Let's start with how to establish a domain name.

Domain Name

Domain names are used to identify the locations of different web pages on the internet. For example, google.com, totalbaseball.com, and iloveblogging.com are all examples of domain names. It is that tiny piece of information that will be used to identify your specific blog.

You will have to find a domain name that is not already taken by someone else. To do this, you can search using sites such as domize.com and instantdomainsearch.com.

Additionally, you should try to create a domain name that is catchy and has at least some of the keywords that you expect people to use when they are searching for blogs similar to yours. In fact, it is best aim for an Exact Match Domain (EMD) which makes it easier to drive traffic to the blog from the search engines (organic traffic). For example, if your site is about epilepsy medication then the EMD would be epilepsymedication.com.

Domain names can be purchased, or they can be obtained for free. An example of a site that offers free domain registry is **www.dot.tk**. If you wish to buy a domain name you can do so through paid webhosting companies such as **www.godaddy.com** and **www.hostgator.com**. Paid webhosting companies usually offer an option for you to purchase a domain name and establish your webhosting right there, on the same site. Moreover, you sometimes have the option of obtaining the domain name for free after paying for the hosting service.

Tips for choosing a domain name

Tip1: When choosing a domain name, do not use the name of a trademarked product or service within it because this may get you into legal trouble with the owners of the copyright or trademark. For example, do not name your domain "dell.jamaica.com" because the word "Dell" is trademarked. Also, remember that you may only use alphanumeric characters and hyphens when naming your domain.

Tip 2: When coming up with your domain name, be mindful of double meanings and hidden words. For example, if you register your domain as "therapistfinder.com," it could be interpreted as "TherapistFinder.com," but to some, it may be read as "TheRapistFinder.com". Therefore, it is important to be careful when choosing your domain name. You can also come up with your own, catchy name that is not necessarily about the specific keyword you are trying to optimize your blog for. No one had ever heard the words Yahoo, Facebook or Google before they came along, and just look at them now – they are household names!

Tip 3: Keep your domain name short. Shorter names are easier to remember than longer ones.

Tip 4: In conjunction with Tip 3, you should avoid using hyphens since these are hard to remember as well.

Tip 5: Do not use numbers on your domain name. They are not only difficult to remember but they are also difficult to explain to people through word of mouth.

Tip 6: Ensure that your domain name is easy to spell. Names that are hard to spell will likely be hard to get right, and therefore, you could easily be driving away traffic.

After obtaining a domain name, the next step you need to take is to host it.

Hosting

You will definitely need a hosting account to put your blog up on the web. Just imagine your dream blog, growing bigger and bigger everyday with more subscribers every second. How would you store the different files that are in your blog? It definitely will not work on your thumb-drive or your hard-drive. Not even an internal and external hard-drive combined is reliable for storing this information. You do not want your site to go offline when power goes off, nor do you want to put these records in jeopardy of viruses or accidental deletion. Your best bet is to have a dedicated hosting service that will do everything for you.

There are two types of hosting: paid hosting and free hosting. The one you choose depends on your specific needs and your reason for blogging. For instance, if you are just blogging for fun then, free hosting may be adequate, but if you plan to blog for reasons other than expressing your creativity, then you might want to consider the disadvantages of free hosting. First, while a free blog would read *yourdomainnamehere.blogspot.com*, a paid hosting blog has the name such as *yourdomainnamehere.com*. Second, with free hosting, you will not have all the features of paid hosting. For example, with free hosting, you are unable to install plug-ins, which may be very helpful for your blog. Additionally, free hosting sites will place whatever advertisements they want on your blog. You do not have any control over which advertisements they choose, nor can you earn money from them.

Additionally, potential customers may be put off by the free hosting and view you as an amateur. It looks more professional in the public's eye to have paid hosting and hence full control over the look and feel of your blog. Moreover, you will not have your own domain but rather a sub-domain which will look unprofessional as well.

Finally, with regard to bandwidth caps, free webhosting will place bandwidth caps on your blog. If your blog is successful and you gain an increasing amount of traffic per day, it is possible that your blog will not be able to handle the amount of visitors to your blog because of the bandwidth caps put in place by your web host. This decreases your blog's reach and, potentially, the income to be made from your blog.

As you can see, with the disadvantages of free hosting, paid hosting is likely be the best bet if you wish to stand out as a professional and make the most out of your blogging efforts. You can host your domain at **Bluehost**, **Go Daddy, iPage**, or **HostGator** to name a few, with prices ranging from approximately $2.25, to$7 based on the added features in each hosting package.

Now that you have a domain name and a webhosting site, the next step is to actually start blogging. In order to do that, you need to choose a platform to blog on. WordPress is the most preferred blogging platform, but another popular option is Blogger.com, which is hosted by Google, the search engine giant. The biggest challenge with blogger is that you will not have as many customization options as you would on WordPress. When you search for WordPress, you might be confused on whether to choose Wordpress.com or WordPress.org. The difference between the two is pretty straightforward.

WordPress.com

On this platform, the sites are free and very easy to setup. Additionally, you can easily customize the theme, but these options are fairly limited. The biggest disadvantage to WordPress.com is that the domain will include ".wordpress.com" at the end, and you will not be able to place ads on the blog. Therefore, if you want a free blog with basic and limited features, choose WordPress.com. The following details how to set up a Wordpress.com blog.

Visit **Wordpress.com** and create an account. You will need to list your preferred blog address here. You can choose "*yourblogaddress.wordpress.com*," which is free, or "*yourblogaddress.com*," which is paid. When you enter your preferred address, Wordpress will let you know whether that address is available for selection or not. The setup process is similar to creating an email account. Simply fill in the details, click "create blog" and confirm your email. Thereafter, you can login to your account using your username and password.

Choose a theme from the free ones available or buy a WordPress theme of your liking. You can find themes on the left side of the menu – click appearance and then themes. When choosing a theme, click "live preview" to get a sense of how it would appear on your site. Then, if you like it, click "save and activate." Alternatively, you can type the theme name if you already know what you want and then click "activate." The design of your blog is now established, and you can begin customizing the design of your posts.

To customize the design of your posts, go to "Settings" and select "General Settings" on the left hand side of the menu. To start with, type the name, otherwise known as the header, for the blog. This is not your blog URL so do not confuse the two. However, can still have the use name if this is what you want your readers to see as the title of open tabs.

Now, you can choose tagline, which is your profession and can be anywhere from an author to accountant or life coach. Then, click "save" located at the bottom of the page. Please note that some themes might need you to upload or choose a background and even upload a header, so just follow the prompts.

Now you can add widgets to your page to enhance both its functionality and its design. To do this, go to "appearance" and select "Widgets." Here, you will be able to select whatever you want your readers to see. Widget options include email subscription – usually referred to as "follow blog" – and social media widgets such as Facebook and Twitter. Other widgets include tag cloud which shows your most used tags), categories, and archives.

Simply grab the widgets by clicking on them, and drag and drop them at the preferred location on your page. You can experiment with different locations until you are fully satisfied. Do not worry about committing to a style because you can always change these later.

Now it is time to add your first blog post. To do this, click on "posts" and select "add new." This will bring you to the "New Post" page.

Tip 1: It is best to write on a different word processor and then copy and paste the text to the "New Post" page. Fill in all of the details on the page, including the title in the "enter title here" section. Once you are done entering all of the details, you can save it as draft or click "publish," after which your first post will go live. You are now a blogger, so continue blogging.

You can also learn more about posting blogs on Wordpress.com.

Tip 2: Bookmark both the front end (i.e. the public pages) and back end (i.e. the administrative view) of your blog for easy access.

WordPress.org

Wordpress.org is where you are able to customize your blog fully the way you want it. This is for the serious blogger who wants to blog, not just for the sake of blogging, but to see returns from his or her efforts. On WordPress.org, you can choose advertisements on your blog, install advanced plugins, and access a large database of themes. It is the ultimate do-it-yourself blogging platform that is fairly easy to set up and gives you the most return from your blogging efforts. Wordpress.org gives you full control of what goes where and how you want your blog to look, which is very critical as a branding tool. Nonetheless, please note that you will be responsible for updating the different plugging manually. This is really just one click, but the fact that it is not automated makes it worth mentioning. To set up a self-hosted WordPress blog, follow the steps below, starting with obtaining a domain name.

If you do not have a domain name yet, you need to obtain a webhosting site. We have already discussed what hosting does, but just to recap, a webhost is basically where the website lives and you pay a small fee for this. Choose a webhost from the list I provided in the previous chapter. From there you can register your domain, which you can buy directly from the hosting company to streamline the process. Bluehost is a great option since you get a free domain when you host your site there.

Now that you have a webhost with a domain name it is time to install Wordpress. The process is pretty straightforward and free. You can opt to install WordPress through your webhosting service, or you can download WordPress on the website and then upload it to your hosting service.

On Wordpress, you need to select a theme for your blog. Although there are several free themes available, you could do better with a premium or custom theme. Once you have your layout established, it is time to log in and start blogging. The process here is just like that of WordPress.com.

Tip 1: Find the administrative side of WordPress.com: yourblogname.com/wp-admin. This is where you click "posts" followed by "add new" to create your first blog.

Knowledge

Before you can begin writing a blog to satisfy the demands of your niche market, you should know what the market desires. If you are already knowledgeable in that area, go ahead and start writing. However, if you do not have sufficient knowledge in the particular field, it is best for you to do thorough research before you begin writing. People will be visiting your blog because you are adding value to them, so make sure you have something useful to tell your audience. This will determine whether they will return to site or not.

Chapter 5:
CreatingContent for Your Blog

When you are done setting up your blog, the next step is to fill in all relevant information so that you present yourself as a professional in whatever you do. No one wants to visit an empty shop! The following steps will guide you through the process of setting up your page professionally.

First, you want to complete the "about us" page as well as the "homepage." This is where you tell the world about yourself as a blogger, the purpose of the blog, and your motivations for creating it. You might want to hire a professional web content writer to craft the content for you.

From there, you should set up a method for capturing email subscribers. Mailchimp is a good place to start since it is free for up to 2000 subscribers. When setting this up, you should ensure that the location of the "opt-in" page is visible to obtain the most subscriptions.

<u>Tip 1:</u> It does not matter how much effort you have put into setting up the blog if you do not share your content], so do not feel inadequate when publishing your first post!

Once you have started posting, do not stop. We already explored the qualities of a successful blogger, but it is important to reiterate that persistence is key if you want to be a success story. Finally, you will need a way to monetize your blog so that you can start profiting from your efforts. Even if you are writing out of passion, earning a few dollars would not be so bad after all! The remaining sections highlight the ways in which you can profit and promote your blog.

Show me the money

The following are a sampling of ways to make money with your blog once it is established.

Affiliate marketing
Affiliate marketing is where you market other people's products on your blog for a commission on every referral made therefrom. There are several options, but the top affiliate marketing networks include Click Bank, Commission Junction, Amazon Affiliates and Share a Sale. You can also try marketing other people's products not listed in these affiliate networks by working

directly with the seller as opposed to affiliate networks that take a commission.

Ad networks (i.e. Cost per click and CPM)

The difference between the Cost per click and CPM is that Cost per click pays for every valid click, while CPM pays for every 1000 impressions. These two advertising networks could make draw in a lot of money if you have a lot of traffic on your site. Popular ad networks include AdSense, AdClickMedia.com and Technoratimedia.com.

Direct ad sales

Direct ad sales are a technique where you sell advertising space to different companies. It is important to note that you will need to have a substantial amount of traffic for people to want to promote their site or services on your blog.

Sell products and services

A final option is for you to sell your own products or services on the blog or use it to promote your offline services. One example is coaching.

Once you have established a means of making money through your blog, the next step is to know how to drive traffic. This is the ultimate determinant of your earnings potential, and the following section shows you how to do it.

How to promote your blog to drive traffic

Commenting on other blogs

One option for promoting your blog is to comment on other people's blogs and leave a link pointing to your blog. However, be careful not to spam people's blogs with "visit my blog" comments. The best practice is to contribute to the discussions in these blogs so that those who read your comment feel the need to check out who you are.

Guest post

Guest posting simply means posting new blog posts on other people's blogs and then leaving a link to your blog. If people like the content you have written, they will feel the need to check out your other posts by visiting your blog.

Blog community sites

These websites can do magic in helping you to market your blog to other bloggers. Top communities include technorati.com and blogcatalog.com. As I previously noted, when you network with other bloggers, you can easily drive traffic in your direction.

Leverage the power of blog directories

To utilize blog directories to your advantage, search "(the topic you blog about) + *directory*" on Google, and you will get a list of directories where you can list your blog.

Tip 1: choose a directory that does not guarantee inclusion since this is the ultimate test of whether the site is legitimate. Some of the best directories include botw.com, blogged.com, greenstalk.com and dir.yahoo.com.

You can also submit your blog to blogcarnival.com for inclusion. You will be amazed by the amount of traffic you can get in the process.

Comment on forums

Your input on forums works in the same manner as blog commenting. Add value to the forum even as you promote your blog through your weblink. People will want to check out your blog when you are contributing informative content to the threads.

Share your content on social networks

With the popularity of social media sites including Facebook and Twitter, you cannot afford to neglect these networks. It is a good idea to include a social media Widget on your blog if you want people to share or like your posts with ease.

Article directories

Sites such as ezinearticles.com and goarticles.com are great avenues for promoting your blog.

Now you are no longer a newbie to the blogging world, and it is time to start blogging consistently and embrace these techniques and qualities. The sky is the limit. The blogging world is constantly changing so you also need to be constantly changing if you are going to stay ahead of the game.

Conclusion

Now that you know what you need to do to blog successfully, you can blog with confidence. Continue reinventing yourself as a blogger if you want to continue blogging long-term and develop a large following. Who knows; you could even end up quitting your day job to concentrate on your blog!

DISCLAIMER AND/OR LEGAL NOTICES: Every effort has been made to accurately represent this book and it's potential. Results vary with every individual, and your results may or may not be different from those depicted. No promises, guarantees or warranties, whether stated or implied, have been made that you will produce any specific result from this book. Your efforts are individual and unique, and may vary from those shown. Your success depends on your efforts, background and motivation.

The material in this publication is provided for educational and informational purposes only and is not intended as medical advice. The information contained in this book should not be used to diagnose or treat any illness, metabolic disorder, disease or health problem. Always consult your physician or health care provider before beginning any nutrition or exercise program. Use of the programs, advice, and information contained in this book is at the sole choice and risk of the reader.

Made in the USA
Lexington, KY
01 June 2015